Introduction

The wok originated in China and is a wide-topped, bowl-shaped metal pan designed for stir-frying small pieces of food in oil or fat over high heat.

Because the frying technique is brisk, all ingredients should be prepared ahead of time and cut into smallish squares or strips, all roughly the same size for even cooking. To retain valuable food nutrients, vegetables should be lightly stir-fried until tender but still crisp in texture and never overcooked. A half rack, which clips over the wok, is available from speciality kitchen shops and is useful for draining as the pictures in the book show. If no similar rack is available, drain food to be reheated on absorbent kitchen paper. Finally, a useful tip: use chopsticks for stirring.

Written by Cornelia Adam

A ....

1 ....

1 i ....

For ....
an ....ey are
no ...erchangeable.

Eggs used are a medium size 3 unless otherwise stated.

For additional hints and tips on wok cooking and the preparation of ingredients, see step-by-step instructions and pictures on pages 18-19 and 34-35.

Kilojoules and kilocalories at the end of each recipe are represented by the letters kJ and kcal.

This edition published 1994 by Merehurst Limited
Ferry House, 51-57 Lacy Road, Putney, London SW15 1PR

Reprinted 1994

Copyright © Gräfe und Unzer GmbH 1993, Munich

ISBN 1 874567 95 6

Designed by Clive Dorman & Co.
Printed in Italy by G. Canale & C.S.p.A

Distributed in the UK by J.B. Fairfax Press Limited,
9 Trinity Centre, Park Farm,
Wellingborough, Northants NN8 6ZB

Distributed in Australia by
J.B. Fairfax Press Pty Ltd,
80 McLachlan Avenue,
Rushcutters Bay,
Sydney, NSW 2011

Lamb with Peppers and Beans

Serves 4

A classic stir-fry combination, well-laced with soy sauce and sherry.

Preparation time: about 25 minutes
Cooking time: 10 minutes

500g (1lb) green beans
Boiling water
Salt to taste
2 medium red peppers (capsicums)
2 medium green peppers (capsicums)
2 medium onions
500g (1lb) boneless fillet of lamb
30g (1oz) fresh parsley
3 tablespoons sunflower or corn oil
4 cloves garlic
60ml (2fl oz/¼ cup) soy sauce
1 tablespoon medium sherry
90ml (3 fl oz/⅓ cup) chicken stock

1 Top and tail beans and remove side strings if necessary. Cut into 1cm (½ in) pieces. Cook beans in boiling salted water for 5 minutes, keeping saucepan two-thirds covered. Drain in a colander. Refresh by rinsing under cold, running water.

2 Halve peppers (capsicums). Remove inner white membranes and seeds. Cut flesh into 1cm (½ in) diamond shapes.

3 Peel and quarter onions. Cut into thin strips.

4 Using a sharp knife, cut lamb into same-sized strips as onions.

5 Wash parsley and shake dry. Coarsely chop.

6 Heat oil in wok until very hot, but not smoking. Add lamb. Stir-fry briskly for 2 minutes. Remove from wok with ladle. Drain on rack or on absorbent kitchen paper.

7 Crush garlic directly into remaining oil in wok. Add beans, peppers and onions. Stir-fry for 3 minutes.

8 Sprinkle soy sauce, sherry and stock over stir-fried ingredients. Return lamb to wok. Reheat until piping hot, stirring. Mix in parsley. Adjust seasoning to taste.

9 Serve with rice, small new potatoes or pasta.

Nutritional value per portion:
about 2000kJ/480kcal
Protein: 32g
Fat: 34g
Carbohydrate: 14g

Lamb with Peppers and Beans

Fried Fish with Rice and Mixed Vegetables

Serves 4

Use favourite fresh or frozen white fish fillets for this unusual stir-fry dish.

Preparation time: about 25 minutes
Cooking time: 15 minutes

220g (7oz/1⅓ cups) long-grain white rice
500ml (16 fl oz/2 cups) boiling water
Salt to taste
2 bulbs fennel
155g (5oz) frozen peas
1 large onion
2 spring onions (green shallots)
750g (1½ lb) skinned white fish fillets, thawed
   if frozen
Fresh lemon juice
2 tablespoons plain flour
2 eggs
3 tablespoons sunflower or corn oil
2 tablespoons medium sherry
3 tablespoons soy sauce
Freshly milled pepper

1 Cook rice in boiling, salted water for 20 minutes. Keep pan tightly covered and heat moderate to prevent water boiling over.

2 While rice is cooking, cut fennel into thin strips. Tip peas on to plate. Peel and quarter onion and cut into thin slices. Trim spring onions (green shallots) and thinly slice.

3 Cut fish into 3.5cm (1½ in) squares. Sprinkle with lemon juice and salt. Tip flour on to piece of non-stick baking paper. Add fish. Coat each piece thoroughly. Beat eggs in bowl until frothy. Add fish and stir until well-covered with egg. Drain on a plate.

4 Heat oil in wok until very hot, but not smoking. Add fish, piece by piece, and stir-fry until golden brown all over. Drain on rack or on absorbent kitchen paper.

5 Add onion slices to remaining oil in wok. Stir-fry for 3 minutes. Add fennel and peas and stir-fry for 5 minutes. Add spring onions (green shallots) and stir-fry for 1 minute.

6 Sprinkle stir-fried ingredients with sherry, soy sauce and pepper. Add salt to taste. Mix in rice, drained if necessary. Top with fried fish cubes. Reheat until hot. Stir carefully, taking care not to break up fish.

Nutritional value per portion:
about 2100kJ/500kcal
Protein: 46g
Fat: 11g
Carbohydrate: 52g

Fried Fish with Rice and Mixed Vegetables

Pork with Mushrooms

Serves 4

Look for dried cloud ear mushrooms in Oriental food shops. Or if preferred, use other dried mushrooms instead.

Preparation time: about 25 minutes
Cooking time: 12-15 minutes

30g (1oz) dried cloud ear mushrooms or
    other dried mushrooms
Boiling water
500g (1lb) pork fillet
Salt to taste
Freshly milled black pepper to taste
4 teaspoons cornflour
155g (5oz) fresh spinach leaves
155g (5oz) fresh bean sprouts
1 medium onion
15g ($\frac{1}{2}$ oz) fresh chives
3 tablespoons soy sauce
2 tablespoons white wine vinegar
125ml (4fl oz/$\frac{1}{2}$ cup) chicken stock
60ml (2fl oz/$\frac{1}{4}$ cup) sunflower or corn oil
1 tablespoon blanched almonds, cut into
    slivers.

1 Rinse mushrooms. Put into bowl. Cover with boiling water and leave for 30 minutes to soak. Tip into sieve. Rinse under cold, running water. Drain thoroughly and cut into small pieces.

2 Cut pork into 1cm ($\frac{1}{2}$ in) strips across the grain. Lightly season with salt and pepper. Sprinkle with 2 teaspoons cornflour and rub well into flesh with fingers.

3 Wash spinach leaves thoroughly to remove grit. Drain well and tear leaves into strips.

4 Rinse bean sprouts under cold, running water. Drain.

5 Peel and finely chop onion. Snip chives into small pieces with kitchen scissors.

6 Mix remaining cornflour with soy sauce, vinegar and stock in small bowl until smooth.

7 Heat oil in wok until very hot, but not smoking. Add pork. Stir-fry briskly for about 3 minutes or until golden brown. Add almonds. Stir-fry with pork for further 1 minute. Remove pork and almonds from wok with ladle and drain on absorbent kitchen paper.

8 Add onion, spinach, bean sprouts and mushrooms to remaining oil in wok. Stir-fry over moderate heat for 4 minutes. Return pork and almonds to wok. Add cornflour mixture and bring to boil, stir-frying continually. Simmer for 2 minutes over low heat. Mix in chives. Adjust seasoning to taste. Serve with rice or pasta.

Nutritional value per portion:
1500kJ/360kcal
Protein: 27g
Fat: 25g
Carbohydrate: 7g

Pork With Mushrooms

Chicken with Wild Rice

Serves 4

Wild rice adds a delicious nutty flavour to this chicken stir-fry.

Preparation time: about 50 minutes
Cooking time: 8-10 minutes

250g (8oz/1½ cups) wild rice
1 litre (1¾ pints/4 cups) boiling water
Salt to taste
500g (1lb) boneless chicken breasts, skinned
1 small onion
2cm (¾ in) fresh root (green) ginger
3 tablespoons snipped fresh chives
90ml (3fl oz/⅓ cup) soy sauce
1 tablespoon dry sherry
1 small cucumber
155g (5oz) fresh or frozen peas
1 medium red pepper (capsicum)
2 eggs
60ml (2 fl oz/¼ cup) sunflower or corn oil

1 Wash rice. Tip into saucepan with boiling water and salt to taste, cover and simmer for 45-50 minutes until grains split open and are tender. Drain if necessary.

2 Cut chicken breasts into thin strips. Transfer to bowl.

3 Peel and finely chop onion. Peel ginger and finely chop. Mix onion and ginger together and combine with chicken. Sprinkle mixture with chives, soy sauce and sherry. Cover and leave to marinate for 30 minutes, stirring occasionally.

4 Peel cucumber, halve lengthwise and remove seeds. Cut flesh into small cubes. Shell peas or thaw frozen ones. Halve pepper (capsicum). Remove inner white membranes and seeds. Cut into small cubes. Beat eggs until frothy.

5 Lift chicken out of marinade with draining spoon. Heat oil in wok until hot, but not smoking. Add chicken and stir-fry briskly for 1 minute. Add prepared vegetables. Stir-fry with chicken for 2 minutes. Take all ingredients out of wok and put on to plate lined with absorbent kitchen paper. Keep warm.

6 Pour eggs into wok. Scramble lightly, stirring continuously, with chop sticks or wooden spoon. Add chicken and vegetables. Reheat for 1 minute. Moisten with soy mixture. Add rice. Continue to stir-fry for about 3 minutes until piping hot. Adjust seasoning to taste. Serve straight away.

Nutritional value per portion:
1800kJ/430kcal
Protein: 47g
Fat: 19g
Carbohydrate: 44g

Chicken with Wild Rice

Chicken with Asparagus

Serves 4

Low in calories, this dish makes an excellent choice for slimmers.

Preparation time: about 15 minutes
Cooking time: 10 minutes

250g (8oz) asparagus spears
Boiling water
Salt to taste
220g (7oz) mange tout (snow peas)
500g (1lb) boneless chicken breasts, skinned
Freshly milled pepper
2 teaspoons cornflour
3 shallots or pickling onions
3 tablespoons sunflower or corn oil
125ml (4 fl oz/½ cup) chicken stock
1 tablespoon medium sherry
2 tablespoons soy sauce
Freshly grated nutmeg to taste
6 sprigs chervil or flat parsley

1 Cut woody ends off asparagus. Cut spears into 2.5cm (1in) pieces. Cook asparagus in boiling salted water for 2 minutes. Drain and rinse under cold water straight away to retain fresh green colour.

2 Top and tail mange tout (snow peas). Cut into diamond shapes.

3 Cut chicken breasts into thin strips. Season lightly with salt and pepper. Transfer to round dish. Sprinkle with cornflour and rub well into flesh with fingers.

4 Peel and finely chop shallots or onions.

5 Heat oil in wok until hot, but not smoking. Add chicken and stir-fry briskly for 1 minute. Remove from wok. Drain on rack or absorbent kitchen paper.

6 Add shallots or onions, asparagus and mange tout (snow peas) to remaining oil in wok. Stir-fry briskly for 1-2 minutes. Add chicken, stock, sherry and soy sauce. Mix thoroughly, cover and simmer for 3 minutes. Return chicken to wok and stir in well. Adjust seasoning to taste. Flavour lightly with nutmeg. Cover and simmer for 2 minutes.

7 Wash and dry chervil or parsley. Take leaves off stalks. Mix into stir-fry.

8 Serve with boiled new potatoes.

Nutritional value per portion:
1000kJ/kcal
Protein: 33g
Fat: 8g
Carbohydrate: 11g

Chicken with Asparagus

Mixed Vegetables with Tofu

Serves 4

A colourful, fiery-flavoured stir-fry, perfect for vegetarians.

Preparation time: about 1 hour
Cooking time: 10 minutes

250g (8oz) firm tofu
3 cloves garlic
5 spring onions (green shallots)
125ml (4fl oz/½ cup) vegetable stock
90ml (3fl oz/⅓ cup) soy sauce
250g (8oz) broccoli
1 large red pepper (capsicum)
1 large yellow pepper (capsicum)
1 medium fresh green chilli
3 tablespoons sunflower or corn oil
Salt to taste
Freshly milled pepper

1 Drain tofu if necessary and cut into 1½ cm (¾ in) pieces. Put on to plate and crush garlic directly over top.

2 Trim spring onions (green shallots) and slice thinly. Sprinkle over tofu with stock and soy sauce. Cover and leave to marinate for1 hour, stirring occasionally.

3 Divide broccoli into small florets. Cut stalks into thin slices. Halve peppers (capsicums). Remove inner white membranes and seeds. Cut flesh into thin strips. Repeat with chilli, wearing rubber gloves to prevent skin burns.

4 Heat oil in wok until hot, but not smoking. Stir in chilli. Lift tofu out of marinade with draining spoon and add to wok. Reserve marinade. Fry tofu briskly until pieces start to turn brown, gently turning. Remove tofu and chilli to bowl.

5 Add pepper (capsicum) strips to remaining oil in wok with broccoli florets and chopped stalks. Stir-fry for 3 minutes. Spoon reserved marinade and spring onions (green shallots) into wok. Bring to boil, stirring, and cook gently for further 3 minutes. Return tofu to wok. Season lightly with salt and pepper and heat through for 2 minutes.

6 Serve with rice or pasta.

Nutritional value per person:
640kJ/150kcal
Protein: 8g
Fat: 9g
Carbohydrate: 9g

Mixed Vegetables with Tofu

Turkey Curry with Celery and Carrots

Serves 4

Unlike most curries, this one takes just minutes to cook.

Preparation time: 15 minutes
Cooking time: 7 minutes

1 medium head celery
315g (10oz) small carrots
500g (1lb) turkey breast fillet
3 tablespoons sunflower or corn oil
Freshly milled pepper
3 teaspoons Korma or Madras curry powder
3 tablespoons soy sauce
125ml (4 fl oz/½ cup) chicken stock
1 tablespoon seedless raisins
Salt to taste

1 Separate celery into sticks, reserving leaves. Remove and discard tough outer strings from each with vegetable knife or peeler. Cut celery into very thin slices. Coarsely chop leaves.

2 Cut carrots into thin slices.

3 Skin turkey breast if necessary. Cut flesh into thin strips.

4 Heat oil in wok until hot, but not smoking. Add turkey breast strips and stir-fry briskly until they start to turn golden. Sprinkle with pepper and curry powder.

5 Add celery and carrots to wok and mix well with turkey. Moisten with soy sauce and stock. Stir in raisins. Simmer for 3 minutes. Adjust seasoning. Sprinkle with chopped celery leaves.

6 Serve with rice or vermicelli noodles (see pages 18-19 on how to prepare).

Nutritional value per portion:
930kJ/220kcal
Protein: 32g
Fat: 8g
Carbohydrate: 6g

Turkey Curry with Celery and Carrots

Step-by step

PREPARING RICE OR VERMICELLI NOODLES

1 Put noodles into large bowl. Cover with boiling water and leave to soak for 5 minutes.

2 Pour into sieve or colander and rinse under cold, running water. Leave to drain.

3 Using kitchen scissors, snip noodles into pieces.

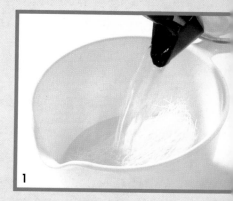

PREPARING MEAT

1 Using sharp knife, cut meat against grain into thin slices.

2 Put meat into dish and dust with cornflour.

3 Rub cornflour well into each slice of beef with finger tips.

PREPARING FRESH ROOT (GREEN) GINGER

1 Thinly peel ginger with a small sharp kitchen knife.

2 Cut into thin slices.

3 Cut each slice into strips and finely chop.

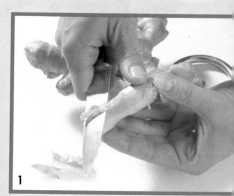

3

3

3

19

Beef Fillet with Bean Sprouts

Serves 4

Strips of beef combined with bean sprouts and spinach.

Preparation time: 20 minutes
Cooking time: 8 minutes

500g (1lb) fillet of beef
1/2 teaspoon cornflour
60ml (2fl oz/¼ cup) sunflower or corn oil
2 cloves garlic
90ml (3fl oz/⅓ cup) soy sauce
155g (5oz) fresh bean sprouts
100g (3½ oz) fresh young spinach
Salt to taste
Freshly milled black pepper to taste
125ml (4 fl oz/½ cup) chicken stock
1 tablespoon medium sherry

1 Cut beef fillet into very thin slices across grain. Sprinkle with cornflour.

2 Heat oil in wok until very hot, but not smoking. Add beef, slice by slice, and stir-fry briskly until browned. Remove from wok with ladle. Drain on rack or on absorbent kitchen paper.

3 Crush garlic into bowl with garlic press. Add soy sauce and mix in meat. Cover and leave to marinate.

4 Rinse bean sprouts under cold, running water. Drain thoroughly.

5 Wash spinach thoroughly to remove grit and drain. Pull leaves off stalks.

6 Add bean sprouts to remaining oil in wok and stir-fry for 1 minute. Add spinach to wok and stir-fry for 2 minutes. Lightly season with salt and pepper. Moisten with stock and sherry.

7 Add beef to wok with soy sauce and ginger mixture and mix in well. Bring to boil and cook for 1 minute. Adjust seasoning to taste.

8 Serve with mixture of brown and wild rice, cooked separately then forked together.

Nutritional value per portion:
1100kJ/260kcal
Protein: 26g
Fat: 14g
Carbohydrate: 4g

Beef Fillet with Bean Sprouts

Chinese Leaves with Ham

Serves 4

The perfect dish for using leftover cooked ham.

Preparation time: 15 minutes
Cooking time: 7 minutes

1 small leek
315g (10oz) Chinese leaves (cabbage)
345g (11oz) cooked ham
2 cloves garlic
2cm (¾ in) fresh root (green) ginger
60ml (2fl oz/¼ cup) sunflower or corn oil
Salt to taste
Freshly milled pepper
1 tablespoon medium sherry
2 teaspoons cornflour
125ml (4 fl oz/½ cup) vegetable stock
3 tablespoons soy sauce

1 Trim leek, slit lengthwise and wash thoroughly under cold, running water to remove grit and mud between layers. Shake dry. Cut into thin rings.

2 Separate Chinese leaves (cabbage). Wash each leaf thoroughly under cold, running water and drain. Cut leaves into thin strips, discarding stalks.

3 Cut ham into thin strips, removing any fat and gristle.

4 Crush garlic on to plate with garlic press. Peel, slice and finely chop ginger.

5 Heat oil in wok until hot, but not smoking. Add ham, garlic and ginger and stir-fry for 1 minute.

6 Mix in leek and strips of Chinese leaves and stir-fry for 5 minutes. Season lightly with salt and pepper. Moisten with sherry.

7 Mix cornflour with stock and soy sauce until smooth. Add to vegetables in wok. Bring to boil. Reheat until piping hot, stirring. Adjust seasoning to taste.

8 Serve straight away with rice or rice noodles.

Nutritional value per portion:
1200kJ/290kcal
Protein: 19g
Fat; 20g
Carbohydrate: 5g

Chinese Leaves with Ham

Chicken Livers with Mushrooms

Serves 4

Use either fresh or dried shiitake mushrooms for this impressive stir-fry.

Preparation time: about 25 minutes
Cooking time: 12 minutes

250g (8oz) fresh shiitake mushrooms or 100g (3½ oz) dried mushrooms
Boiling water for dried mushrooms
500g (1lb) chicken livers
2 teaspoons cornflour
Pinch of salt
Freshly milled pepper
½ teaspoon caster sugar
2 tablespoons medium sherry
75ml (2½ fl oz/⅓ cup) soy sauce
1 medium onion
345g (11oz) small courgettes (zucchini)
60ml (2 fl oz/¼ cup) sunflower or corn oil
30g (1oz) blanched almonds, cut into slivers
75ml (2½ fl oz/⅓ cup) chicken stock

1 Wipe fresh mushrooms clean with soft cloth or absorbent kitchen paper. Cut into thin strips. If using dried mushrooms, put into bowl, cover with boiling water and leave to soak for 30 minutes. Drain and wipe dry. Cut into strips, discarding stems.

2 Wash and dry livers, see pages 34-35. Cut into small pieces and toss with cornflour in bowl.

3 Make marinade by mixing together salt, pepper, sugar, sherry and soy sauce. Mix marinade into livers, cover and leave to stand for 10 minutes.

4 Peel and halve onion. Cut each half into thin slices. Top and tail courgettes (zucchini) and slice very thinly with sharp knife or on side of grater.

5 Heat oil in wok until hot, but not smoking. Add almonds and stir-fry until just beginning to brown, watching carefully as they quickly burn. Add onion, courgettes (zucchini) and mushrooms and stir-fry for 5 minutes. Remove from wok with draining spoon and put into bowl.

6 Lift livers out of marinade. Add to remaining oil in wok. Stir-fry briskly for 3 minutes. Mix in vegetables and almonds. Add stock and marinade. Bring to boil, then simmer for 1 minute. Adjust seasoning to taste.

7 Serve with rice or vermicelli noodles.

Nutritional value per portion:
1300kJ/310kcal
Protein: 31g
Fat: 16g
Carbohydrate: 8g

Chicken Livers with Mushrooms

Rice noodles with Prawns

Serves 4

This stir-fry is delicious eaten cold and makes a wonderful buffet dish.

Preparation time: 10 minutes
Cooking time: 5 minutes

100g (3½ oz) rice or vermicelli noodles
Boiling water
250g (8oz) celery sticks
2 spring onions (green shallots)
250g (8oz) carrots
1 fresh green chilli
60ml (2fl oz/¼ cup) sunflower or corn oil
3 cloves garlic
315g (10oz) cooked peeled prawns, thawed
    if frozen
2 tablespoons medium sherry
3 tablespoons soy sauce
90ml (3 fl oz/⅓ cup) vegetable stock
Pinch of salt
Pinch of caster sugar

1 Put noodles into large bowl, cover with boiling water and leave to stand for 5 minutes. Tip into colander and rinse under cold, running water. Using kitchen scissors, snip noodles into shortish lengths. Drain thoroughly.

2 To prepare celery, cut off green leaves and reserve. Remove and discard tough outer strings from each celery stick with kitchen knife. Slice celery thinly. Coarsely chop leaves.

3 Trim spring onions (green shallots). Cut into 1cm (½ in) pieces.

4 Halve carrots lengthwise. Cut each half into thin slices.

5 Wearing rubber gloves, slit chilli lengthwise. Remove seeds with knife and finely chop flesh.

6 Heat oil in wok until hot. Crush garlic directly into hot oil. Add celery, spring onions (green shallots) and carrots. Stir-fry for 1 minute.

7 Mix in noodles and prawns. Stir-fry for 1 minute. Add sherry, soy sauce, stock, salt, sugar and chopped chilli and mix thoroughly. Heat through until piping hot. Sprinkle with chopped celery leaves and serve straight away.

Nutritional value per portion:
1200kJ/290kcal
Protein: 20g
Fat: 11g
Carbohydrate: 25g

Rice noodles with Prawns

Pork with Broccoli

Serves 4

A colourful combination of vegetables and pork.

Preparation time: about 20 minutes
Cooking time: 14 minutes

220g (7oz) carrots
315g (10oz) broccoli
100g (3½ oz) mushrooms
1cm (½ in) fresh root (green) ginger
500g (1lb) pork fillet
Salt to taste
Freshly milled black pepper to taste
1 tablespoon cornflour
60ml (2fl oz/¼ cup) sunflower or corn oil
2 cloves garlic
3 tablespoons soy sauce
125ml (4fl oz/½ cup) chicken stock
Pinch of caster sugar
3 tablespoons snipped fresh chives

1 Cut carrots into very thin slices. Separate broccoli into small florets. Thinly slice broccoli stalks.

2 Wipe mushrooms with absorbent kitchen paper and trim stalks. Thinly slice. Peel ginger, slice thinly and finely chop.

3 Cut pork into thin slices against grain. Season lightly with salt and pepper. Sprinkle with cornflour. Rub well into pork with finger tips.

4 Heat oil in wok until hot, but not smoking. Add pork. Stir-fry briskly for 1 minute. Remove with draining spoon on to rack or absorbent kitchen paper.

5 Add carrots, broccoli and mushrooms to remaining oil in wok and stir-fry for 1 minute. Crush garlic directly into the hot oil. Add ginger. Sprinkle with soy sauce and stock and mix in sugar. Cover and simmer for 5 minutes.

6 Return pork to wok and mix thoroughly with vegetables. Cover and simmer for 5 minutes. Sprinkle with chives.

7 Serve with curry-flavoured rice.

Nutritional value per portion:
1300kJ/310kcal
Protein: 30g
Fat: 18g
Carbohydrate: 6g

28

Pork with Broccoli

Minced Beef with Savoy Cabbage

Serves 4

A hearty stir-fry ideal for cold winter months.

Preparation time: about 15 minutes
Cooking time: 15 minutes

315g (10oz) Savoy cabbage
1 large onion
250g (8oz) oyster mushrooms
60ml (2fl oz/¼ cup) sunflower or corn oil
3 cloves garlic
500g (1lb) lean minced beef
Salt to taste
Freshly milled pepper to taste
Paprika to taste
3 tablespoons soy sauce
125ml (4fl oz/½ cup) beef stock
Pinch of caster sugar

1 Separate cabbage leaves and remove pieces of hard stalk from each. Wash leaves well, drain throughly and shred with sharp knife.

2 Peel and halve onion and cut each half into thin slices.

3 Wipe mushrooms with absorbent kitchen paper, but do not wash. Cut flesh into thin strips.

4 Heat oil in wok until very hot, but not smoking. Add onion and stir-fry fairly gently until they begin to look transparent. Crush garlic directly into the hot oil.

5 Mix in beef and stir-fry briskly until brown and crumbly. Season generously with salt, pepper and paprika. Remove to bowl with draining spoon.

6 Add cabbage to remaining oil in wok and stir-fry for 4 minutes.

7 Add mushrooms to wok and mix well with cabbage. Stir-fry for 5 minutes. Moisten with soy sauce and stock. Add sugar and adjust seasoning.

8 Return beef to wok and combine with vegetables. Reheat until hot.

9 Serve with long grain rice.

Nutritional value per portion:
1600kJ/380kcal
Protein: 33g
Fat: 26g
Carbohydrate: 7g

Minced Beef with Savoy Cabbage

Squid with Vegetables and Sesame Seeds

Serves 4

Squid combined with Chinese leaves and crunchy sesame seeds.

Preparation time: about 15 minutes
Cooking time: 20 minutes

315g (10oz) Chinese leaves (cabbage)
1 large tomato
500g (1lb) ready-prepared squid (calamari)
   or octopus rings
3 tablespoons soy sauce
2 tablespoons white wine vinegar
3 tablespoons crème fraîche
Salt to taste
Freshly milled pepper
Pinch of sugar
3 tablespoons sunflower or corn oil
3 tablespoons sesame seeds
4 tablespoons fresh chopped dill

1 Separate cabbage leaves. Remove pieces of hard stalk from each. Wash leaves well and drain thoroughly. Shred cabbage with sharp knife.

2 Cover tomato with boiling water for 30 seconds, then plunge into cold water and peel away skin. Cut tomato into slices.

3 Rinse squid (calamari) or octopus under cold, running water.

4 Make sauce by mixing together soy sauce, vinegar and crème fraîche. Season with salt, pepper and sugar.

5 Heat oil in wok until very hot, but not smoking. Add squid (calamari) or octopus and stir-fry briskly for 5 minutes. Add sesame seeds and fry for 1-2 minute with fish. Season with salt, pepper and sugar. Lift out of wok with draining spoon on to absorbent kitchen paper.

6 Reduce heat. Add Chinese leaves (cabbage) and tomato to remaining oil in wok. Half cover and simmer for 8 minutes. Stir in soy sauce mixture and stir-fry until bubbling. Return fish and sesame seeds to wok and mix in well. Cover and simmer for 5 minutes over moderate heat. Adjust seasoning to taste.

7 Sprinkle dill over stir-fried ingredients.

8 Serve with rice to which gound ginger has been added while cooking.

Nutritional value per portion:
1000kJ/240kcal
Protein: 22g
Fat: 16g
Carbohydrate: 4g

Squid with Vegetables and Sesame Seeds

Step-by step

COOKING MEAT IN WOK

1 Heat oil in wok until hot and sizzling, gently swirling it round to cover sides. Cut meat, poultry, fish or vegetables (or combination) into even-sized pieces and add to wok.

2 Spread out with ladle or metal spatula and stir-fry until browned and evenly cooked.

3 Drain food to be reheated later on rack attached to wok. Alternatively, put on to absorbent kitchen paper and keep warm.

1

PREPARING CHICKEN LIVERS

4 Remove gristle and fat from livers.

5 Cut livers into bite-sized pieces.

6 Coat with cornflour.

4

PREPARING A CHILLI

7 Slit chilli lengthwise.

8 Remove seeds with knife from chilli.

9 Cut chilli into narrow rings. Wash hands well.

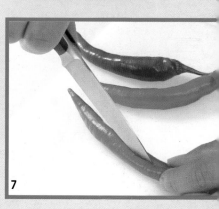

7